UNDERESTIMATED BY YOU!

RAVI RANA

ISBN 979-888530658-4

I dedicate this book to my parents, family and my mentors
for always supporting all my dreams and inspiring my
thoughts to the best of my limits.

Contents

Prologue

Youths are the leaders of tomorrow. We can't deny that this young generation will play a crucial role in building our nation. But are most teenagers aware of the critical problems of the world? Do they know what they will be handling when they are old enough? Do they know what our world is suffering through or what important movements are going on to bring ultimate peace and consider our countries as a whole nation?

Don't worry, neither did I until I started using the internet for my conversance.

Browsing the internet, you come across various topics and various points of view regarding those topics, but the important thing is to have a point of view of your own. Not everything has to be 100% accurate, but we can brainstorm solutions to some problems and spread our knowledge to change the world. Maybe it will work? Or it wouldn't? But the thing that really matters is that you tried!

I know most of you will be like "who reads this kind of book anyway?" but trust me if you don't read it you'll be regretting it, and ruining the ideas that your brain could've come up with for the problems we all are facing.

You will know more about these topics and have a great conversation with anyone anywhere!

I am writing this book from my perspective on some problems and how these problems are misunderstood and underestimated by the world.

Being a 14-year-old, I may not have all the knowledge about these topics, but I hope you can relate to my point of view and have your own different opinions on these topics. I hope it gives you the awareness that I aim to deliver.

Being aware of your surroundings will help you be an essential part of the bright tomorrow. So what are you waiting for? START RIGHT NOW! Discover the problems you want to get rid of before they wreck the world even more.

CHAPTER ONE

YOU KNOW YOURSELF BETTER

Nowadays, society and media have trained you to look at some people in a certain way through images on Instagram, magazines, TV, banners, and everywhere. These people include those who don't fit in with the "unrealistic" and "photoshopped" beauty standards set by the media. The media with the help of society spreads these "perfect" images of what an individual should ideally look or be like, which makes us see "less perfect" people with judgemental eyes. This is what bullying is, one of the most underrated obstacles in the evolution of our community.

A dangerous number of people are a victim of bullying, even though you may not realize but you are being bullied when someone asks you to change something about yourself to "fit in" with the standards of society, you being are bullied when people look at you with a certain outlook without even knowing you, you are being bullied when a certain comments affect your mental health and you are being bullied when you start hating yourself because of others.

A huge number of people are missing out on their lives by simply running away and hiding from their oppressors. They are throwing their lives because of a tyrant, who is making them suffer physically and mentally. It's nothing compared to the people, including young adults, committing suicide due to the malicious act of bullying.

It's a much bigger problem than we realize and we, as a community, need to unite in order to fight bullying. We need to intervene in other's matters more and try to find out what problems are they facing and help them overcome their struggles. Bullies are also somewhat the victims, seeking power when they can't get enough at their own safe place but their behaviour should not be encouraged just because they feel neglected.

Your friends, teachers, or peers cannot always be there to save you from bullies but you always have yourself. Stick to the trait that you love about yourself, it's hard considering we are our own biggest detractor. You know yourself way better than anyone else. Don't let anyone tear you down. Just be yourself and don't let anyone tell you otherwise.

There's no way to stop bullying other than standing up for yourself. You don't need to ask people to change the little flaws within them but what you do need to teach them is how to accept yourself with those little flaws and be confident in your own skin. Make yourself emotionally and physically stronger with the support of the people who love you and don't let anybody, I repeat anybody, bring you down.

My advice to some people reading this is,

If you are a parent, try to talk with your children, understand what they are going through, don't intervene and try to find all the solutions to their problems because they find it annoying and won't tell you anything from then, validate their feelings, tell them that it's okay to feel the way they are feeling, Support them and let them fight their own battles by giving them the strength they need.

If you are a bully, my only advice to you is, you don't know what the other person is going through, you don't know how one sentence/comment from you can lead someone's heart to shatter, someone to cry, someone to end their own life, someone to isolate themselves from the world, it's a request to please monitor your words and actions and constrain your aggressiveness.

Each day a new story of bullying rises, which is ignored by us thinking it's just another story. The thing that we need to understand is that those voices which are gone, those names which are forgotten, and the stories that are ignored, all matter.

We all need to have determination as individuals and as a community to take actions that make a difference. As a great personality once said, "YOU must be the change YOU wish to see in the world."

CHAPTER TWO

ARE WE EQUAL?

Many things in this world are misunderstood by us. One of them is feminism.

Feminism, a word derived from French, means a range of movements or ideologies that define equality of the sexes at all levels. Feminism is fighting for the equal rights of every gender, whether it be men or women. Feminists do not withhold any concealed desires to disseminate women's domination, nor do they want any special perquisites for them.

The entire point of feminism is to welcome decisions and be anything one wants to be without judging another person on their preferences. Everyone should be free to do whatever they want and look however they fancy.

You may be thinking that now the world has been modernized, what problem could a person even face based on their gender? But you, my friend, are very wrong. There are a ton of problems, we all deal with but are too busy to point out.

I don't know how many of you noticed but I think Harry Potter also portrayed the message of feminism as the female lead was standing up for herself and her choices during a time when women were highly oppressed by the male society and were not allowed to speak up for themselves.

Let me list out a few examples for you,

Why are people trolled for wearing makeup? If you wear makeup, you are regarded as a cake face, and if you don't, your natural beauty comes across as ugly. Why is a women's dressing style judged? Why are the men hated for wearing "feminine" clothes? If a person wants, he/she can dress however they like, a woman can dress masculine, a man can wear feminine clothes, it is their choice to dress however they want, but society judging them is depriving them of their human rights. Some very serious problems that revolve around the issue of feminism include the Right to Abortion in every country, the vanishing of domestic violence, end of a stereotyped and gender-biased society.

Now moving onto the topic of particularly women,

As we all know, women have always been in the minority division, they have been underestimated throughout their living, we are all aware of the patriarchal society we live in, we are well aware of the discrimination that takes place against the women, we are aware of the differences the women face, we are aware of the fact that women earn less for the same job in comparison to men, but do we do anything about it? Most probably not. Feminism is liberating the idea of equality of rights and entitlement, gender roles, across all social divisions, asking for a just and equitable society encompassing everyone.

Feminism fights against stereotyping, control over the movements of an individual, and gives everyone the equal right that they deserve.

From their childhood years, boys are, asked to be strong, brave, made to think that they are superior and that they are going to lead the world. They are taught to be the "alpha" men.

Girls, on the other hand, are asked to be subdued, gentled, and not argumentative, they are told not to gain more muscles as they would look masculine, they are told to dress a certain way. Furthermore, their movements are controlled, they are asked to have a certain friendzone, They have a certain period of lockdown to remain "safe". They can't roam around the streets at night because of the fear of something bad happening to them.

Imagine thinking a victim is blamed for the crime that they have encountered. Well, it's true. Most of the women are blamed when a crime against them takes place because apparently, they did not follow the rules imposed on them by society.

"We must raise our daughters differently. We must also raise our sons differently."

— Chimamanda Ngozi Adichie

So let me ask you a question, Why should biological differences lead to different social statuses? They shouldn't! And that's what feminism is trying to convey, it's a universal beauty that's fighting for equal opportunities for the sexes.

"WE need feminism because a man in a room of women is ecstatic. A woman in a room full of men are terrified"

An important thing that I felt the need to mention here is gender roles,

"Gender roles should be a matter of choice not compulsion"

Everyone should have the right to decide the roles they want to play and no one can force those roles on anybody just because they are a woman or a man. A man raising a child, a woman being the breadwinner of a family, women going to the gym, and many more should not be criticized.

Now you might want to ask me my views to help you contribute to this struggle,

Well as Emma Watson, one of the most powerful women that I know, once said, Gender equality is not only the issue of women but of men also. According to my opinion, men should also be an equal part of this struggle as much as women, it should be their problem too, they shouldn't fear the views of society and help support a great cause.

I would like all the females here to just do whatever they can to voice the injustice they feel is going around, even the smallest things can make a big difference.

And as for the guys, I only want you to listen the what we females have to say, you have to try and put yourself in our shoes and look at the world from a different perspective.

If questioning patriarchy, questioning the control men have, questioning the denial of education of women, questioning the denial of equal salary wages, questioning the denial of equal skill-building opportunities for women, and questioning gender equality as a whole makes me a feminist than I AM A FEMINIST and you should be too! Nobody has any right to call a feminist just an angry individual because if fighting for equal rights and opportunities makes us "angry" women then everyone should be angry because gender equality is the issue of all sexes.

"The fact that you have to explain what feminism is, is the reason we need feminism"

THIS NEEDS TO BE ADDRESSED!

Teenage is the most vulnerable period in the life of a human. Teen depression is a rising medical illness. It's more than just a feeling of being glum or "blue" for a few days. It is an intense feeling of sadness, hopelessness, and anger or frustration that lasts much longer. These feelings make it hard for you to function normally and do your usual activities. You may also have trouble focusing and have no motivation or energy. Depression can make you feel like it is hard to enjoy life or even get through the day. Teens nowadays have much exposure to social media that leads them to compare themselves with unrealistic standards set by influencers, it degrades our self-esteem and makes them troubled with themselves causing them to go into a dark state of mind and even consider self-harm as an option. We, Teenagers, have our whole life and career ahead of us so we have a lot of pressure on us to make the right career choice ourselves, in this age, most teens are not aware of their goals in life so which leads them to doubt themselves.

Being a teen, I feel like we are just lost in a sea full of thoughts about everything, we feel isolated from the real world and that feeling just took a bigger toll when the pandemic struck, our golden year just went by, without us knowing what to do and whom to talk to. I agree that we have our parents but they are not able to relate to us the same way kids our age can, they would be too busy questioning our feelings and giving us needless solutions.

Teenage is all about experimenting and coming across various things, during this experimenting, we fail, we pass and we learn. But out of all those things we focus only on the times we failed and bring our self-esteem down to zero.

In this era, all the kids feel like they need to fit in amongst the social circle and maintain their reputation to not be excluded from all the activities and not get bullied. Studies have also confirmed that most teenagers go into depression because they are afraid of not fulfilling all of the high expectations their peers or parents have for them.

Teens also fear rejection and judgment in voicing out their opinions or feelings, this causes us to bottle up our emotions, and then just hate on ourselves for not standing up. comparing ourselves to other people makes us feel less proud of the small achievements that we are making.

Some of the teens also suffer from social anxiety due to having experienced mental or physical trauma during childhood.

Teenagers going through depression may start relying on drugs, alcohol, vape to cope up with their feelings which is called substance abuse. This substance abuse is totally not okay because it risks the life of teens who are the future blocks of our nation.

During teenage, our emotions and hormones are on a giant rollercoaster, but we don't have anybody besides us to overcome this ride and that's the worst phase of all.

I think communication is the key to everything so if you know or are somebody battling depression just know that you're not the only one and that you've someone who understands who you feel. Please just talk with your know ones, ask them to open up about their feelings when they are ready to face it, and just validate them that it's okay to feel that way and there's nothing wrong with them feeling those things because sometimes we just need somebody to talk to and you lending an ear to someone may help in ways you might not even know.

In conclusion, depression in teens is very ordinary nowadays due to exposure and the way of living they have but it can only be healed with correct guidance and support. Teens don't need to rely on drugs and other substances to overcome depression. As it is already becoming big, we need to spread as much awareness about it as possible so people don't treat mental health as a taboo topic anymore and seek the correct cure for it. Methods to fight depression include talk therapy, also called psychotherapy or counselling, which can help them understand and manage their moods and feelings. Medicines like antidepressants are also suggested by therapists. Some teens who have severe depression or are at risk of hurting themselves may need more intensive treatment. They may go into a psychiatric hospital or do a day program. Both of these programs contain counselling sessions with mental health specialists.

The most important thing that can cure you of depression is the support of your friends and family and your own mindset of fighting this battle. Remember it's okay to be ill but it's not okay to remain ill.

CHAPTER FOUR

A SKILL WE ARE USELESS WITHOUT

Self-confidence is a skill, a skill that you're useless without, a skill that helps you achieve your goals, a skill that'll make you a great leader, a skill that'll help you achieve your goals against all the odds and adversities you might face, it's a skill that only you can build.

We expect to be self-confident but we can't be unless we are aware of the lack of it.

We can't expect to be self-confident unless it's a thing that we've done a thousand times. And doing things, again and again, is also a brave task to do because many of us tend to bail at our first attempts only, we don't even see the point in trying after we fail once. We need to teach ourselves how to NOT accept failure, don't accept NO and keep going on, be persistent.

"our thoughts influence our actions so think positively because there's nothing that you cant do and you just need to keep affirming that to yourself"

Remember this, I'm not telling you to remove the negative

thoughts from your head because the more you focus on removing those thoughts, the more you'll be thinking about them, they'll be taking up more of your time and tearing down the confidence that you've built up. I'm just asking you to focus on the positive vibes, the optimistic self-affirmations, the positive self talk because focusing on them will make you more aware of all the good things in your life that you'll forget about all the negatives going around.

They are already enough people criticising you, you don't need to be another critic for your own self because guess what? you are the only one you really have.

We need to overcome the negative thoughts that go on in our head, underestimating our worth, telling us we are not good enough and trying to run away from the problem instead of just simply facing it. What will be the big deal if you just face the problems? The most that'll happen is that you'll fail but failure will teach you a lesson and your persistence will keep you going on and on until you conquer the problem. Trying to run away from that problem you'll do yourself more harm than good, you'll not be able to know your mistakes, there will be no scope of correction in that, and you'll not be able to run away from those problems for a lifetime. Will you? No right! By trying to avoid failure you'll also be avoiding success!

So instead of trying to run away just put yourself out there, doesn't matter if it's right or wrong, and evolve, challenge yourself to do better next time, because there's always a next time.

"if you don't believe yourself, no one else will
if you don't love yourself, no one else will
if you are not proud of yourself, no one else will be

if you don't remind yourself what you are capable of, no one else will
if you let yourself down, everyone else will"

you need to cut off the people who are tearing you down, who are criticising you for being happy, who are holding you back from achieving YOUR goals because you don't want that in your life. All you need is positive self-affirmation and positive energy to keep you going through the storm.

We are the people who create values in the world, we are the people who need to spread all the things we have onto other people. Instead of pointing out the things that one does wrong and applaud them for the things they did right because they already know what they did wrong and if they don't, you to give them examples by encouraging the ones who did it right and in return, they'll feel more motivated to do better next time.

This is a thing only you can build for yourself but you sure can pass it on to others and make them feel just a little more confident about them selves.

CHAPTER FIVE

NOW OR LATER?

We are busy criticizing other people, envying them for "having it all" instead of just trying to improve ourselves and empower ourselves. Our negative mentality keeps on revolving around us, bringing us down.

Our actions show that we believe criticizing others is better than self-evolving, but that's not right. Blooming and evolving yourself will benefit you as well as your surroundings because you will give in the best input you possibly can by being the best version of yourself and evolving throughout your life, which will result in society giving out a better output for you and other people. I'm not saying the betterment of the whole society depends on you but I am saying you are capable of making society better just by being finer than you were yesterday.

But we find being the weaker person easier because why not? You just have to envy all your friends, compare their life to your miserable life, be stuck in the same mental and emotional place that's going to degrade every day. Your body, mind, and spirit will be plagued in the forms of phobias, addictions, anxieties, fear, and physical disease. It's a lot easier than just putting yourself in a better place, accepting your flaws, Being confident enough to do anything, moving on, and achieving your goals by becoming your best version.

Life is all about evolving, animals evolve unconsciously, humans have to evolve consciously because they have the freedom to be whoever they want. We believe that we also grow unconsciously as day by day our height and weight increase but does our mental health strengthen with time too? No right! When you can be whoever you want, you have that freedom with you, why waste the opportunity when you can make it count?

You, if you want, can be the best existing version of yourself, just by competing with yourself from yesterday, doing things a little better than yesterday, focusing on yourself a little more, and being closer to your definition of success.

By your definition of success, I mean the goals you aim to achieve in life because success has a different meaning for each of us. Some people's success may be based on their families, others' success may be based on money and business while the left people maybe define success as exploring various things and travelling around the globe.

What we are doing wrong here is that we are not even accepting the fact that we can be better, we comfort ourselves into thinking that everything is fine by giving examples of people dying from cancer, diabetes, and whatnot. We delude ourselves into thinking that we already have enough money while looking at the people who can't even afford to have two meals a day. And that obviously does make us seem perfect in our heads. We are better than those people but self-evolution refers to your own evolving process,

'Are you better than the "YOU" yesterday'

Ask yourself this!

The goal of self-evolution is just to be a little better "you" than yesterday. The journey of self-evolution starts from facing ourselves, knowing what we are doing. Then it comes down to accepting the fact that there are some things that we are doing wrong and some things which we are doing right. In the end, comes evolving, according to me the hardest part was accepting your flaws and strengths, just accepting myself in general, evolving had a bit to do with the mental self - talk, evolving became easy when I identified my flaws and praised my strengths, that way I knew what to improve, just implementing them became a bit of a tedious task but trust me if you think you can do it, you CAN do it!

Furthermore, self-evolution helps us define our goals better, it gives value to our success,

We all know the importance of making ourselves better and not missing out on life but sometimes all we need is a push, a little motivation to stop being a coward and stand up to be the best we can ever be. It's all you can ever do it's the change in you, making you better or just accepting yourself and being the same person you are throughout your life.

Bringing a small change with every conscious moment of our life would be better than remaining the same and hating yourself after some time passes, it would be better than underestimating your strengths, it would be better than your own self tearing you down, and it would be better than getting fed up with who you really are. It would be better if you could be just a little more aware, a little more generous, a little more knowledgable, a little more skilled. It's either this small change or unconditional love and acceptance towards yourself but that may turn into self-ignorance sometimes when we know there's something wrong with us and we can fix it but we are okay with

it. why? because we love ourselves. That's pure ignorance which may cost you a lot.
It's up to you, you will always have a choice, change now or later? Because you'd have to change eventually.

CHAPTER SIX

THIS IS NOT OKAY!

"The world will not be destroyed by those who do evil, but by those who watch them without doing anything."

Albert Einstein

How many things are happening or are continuing to happen just because we turn a blind eye to them?! We, instead of speaking up, are encouraging serious issues by keeping quiet. You are gifted with a voice to put yourself forward, to support the causes you believe in, to add power and strength to the voices of others.

One of the things you might know very little about is "Racism". Racism is the thought that features and capabilities can be attributed to people merely based on their race and that some racial groups are superior to others.

Racism isn't just discrimination having a prejudiced attitude based on faulty presumptions about distinct ethnicities. Racism involves power, the mastery to dictate and govern outcomes. This power is exerted by the elite groups which harm and restrict the activities of people of colour to enjoy their social, political and monetary advantages.

Racism, according to me is, When a privileged group of people exerts authority over another group based on skin colour and perceived differences between races. This racism corrupts every level of our society. Racism is like a toxin that's antagonising every level of our community.

Let me ask you a question

Is being colourblind okay? By this I mean, not addressing people's colour and just turning a blind eye to all the races, Is it okay according to you?

According to my opinion, it's not because if we don't acknowledge the race of other people, we'll be overlooking the injustices taking place against certain people. We must acknowledge all the colours to find a way out of the troubles that coloured people face.

I don't know why, but it seems like all the minority ethnicities can be wiped off as scapegoats for the majority, the same thing flourished its way in the society under the rule of Hitler.

I'm not gonna list all the examples of racism taking place all over the globe but I am going to give you an overview of the stances of our nation about racism.

Europe has had a big history of racism including malicious acts against immigrants, minoritics that even escalated to violent racism.

In Australia, races were used to gain political support, people were turned against each other for a political party to win, people also did face racism during the Olympics, racist attacks and lynching even took place against Indians.

We all know about the apartheid struggle in Africa but Africa also did face discrimination against white farmers just because some non-residents promoted ethnic hatred and differences.

In the middle east, there is a whole tornado of racism going around, people of colour face discrimination at work and away from work, they are often not permitted at some beaches or clubs or are allowed with various restrictions. In addition, property rights are severely curtailed, even Palestinians faced discrimination who are of the same race, but not nationals. There were some acts of terrorism associated with racism too.

In Asia, there has been racism, fighting between different ethnicities and castes because some people are held responsible for the economic plague in some countries, some country's hate other ethnicities because they want their culture to be favoured the most, the lower casts face prejudice and many more.

North America also has a horrific history of racism including the 9/11 attack.

Now you all got an overview of how all of us suffered because of this vicious act of racism but this was not the end though it became less for some time but it's growing once again.

From George Floyd's horrifying murder to the police brutality and the institutional racism that has paved its way to persist.

We are now aware of another movement #BlackLivesMatter #BLM!! Why did we need it in the first place? Why didn't this movement come to an end right after 2013, when it was launched? You're right, that's because we didn't pay enough attention to it. After all, it was not our lives on the stake, now was it?

The BLM movement is continuing to play a prominent role in demonstrations against police brutality and racism.

Institutionalized racism and abuse of power are a problem in the USA, but that does not mean that we all cant fight against it and bring all the violence and discrimination to an end.

"If we stick together, we can do anything"

To overcome racism, we need to understand it from the perspective of the people who are suffering and identify our privileges whether it be a socio-economic privilege, whether it be a gender-based privilege or any other. After being aware of your privileges, engage in tough conversations about race and injustice with people of colour too. Ask them how they are feeling about the discrimination going on against them, put yourself in their shoes, and validate their feelings, tell them that it's okay to feel the way they are feeling, and help them cope with any issue they might have. By putting yourself in theirshoes, you'll be more aware of their feelings and the discrimination that takes place against them, this will help you stand up against the injustice better. If somebody makes racist remarks or jokes point them out, whether it be in real life or social media because small steps lead to big changes. Try and spread more awareness about these things among your friends and family.

"your ethnicity, your culture, your colour and YOU
are to be cherished,
not to be hated upon"

CHAPTER SEVEN

AT LAST OR START?

I hope you enjoyed reading about all the problems we as a society are facing and now you are aware of what you can do to support your cause. Everyone has their own story and maybe that story has occurred a million times but it still hasn't been spoken by you! Your own voice does matter and you need to use it for the right cause! I hope you all were inspired to make your peers, siblings, parents or even mentors aware of these things. These are just the normal things that we know, we face every day.

SUPPORT EACH VOICE BECAUSE EVERY VOICE MATTERS!

" There are problems here and there,
Even if we solve one,
we'll be the kind bear "

Our problems don't end here and nor do their solutions. So we'll see if it's the end of this book or the start of another. Peace!

About The Author

Ravi Rana is a teenager who hails from New Delhi, India. She loves supporting social causes and lending a helping hand to others, making them aware of society's problems. She believes "awareness is the greatest agent for change."